A Teacher's Guide to
Sefer Ha-Aggadah

The Book of Legends for Young Readers
Volume 1: Bible Legends

Ellen Singer

UAHC Press • New York

This book is printed on acid-free paper.
Copyright © 1997 by the UAHC Press
Manufactured in the United States of America
10 9 8 7 6 5 4 3 2 1

Contents

	Introduction: A Letter to Educators	v
1	Light and Fire	1
2	How Shall You Be Blessed?	5
3	What Is a Promise Worth?	8
4	Loving the Small Things	12
5	A Time to Pray, A Time to Act	15
6	God's Marvelous Voice	18
7	Shall There Be One Law for Man and Another for Woman?	21
8	Deborah, Woman of Light	25
9	King David Studies Torah	28
10	Solomon and the Snake	31
11	A Hundred Hidden Prophets	34
12	Jeremiah and Moses	38

Introduction

Dear Educator,

A story can be a very powerful teaching tool. Long before there was printing (much less the electronic communication of today), there were stories. The Jewish Bible is one of the first great repositories of stories. The sages of Jewish history, in particular those of the talmudic era, expanded, enriched, and embellished the biblical tales, creating a genre known as the *aggadah*. *Aggadah* literally means "legend," but for the rabbis and sages of the past these legends were more than a means of entertainment. Each *aggadah* sought to convey a message, to teach a lesson.

Sefer Ha-Aggadah: The Book of Legends for Young Readers is a deftly written adaptation of the classic *Sefer Ha-Aggadah*, "The Book of Legends." The original classic grew out of the desire of two men, Hayim Nahman Bialik and Yehoshua Hana Ravnitzky, to bring ancient Hebrew to life as a modern language. They collected the legends and stories of the sages of talmudic times and presented them in Hebrew. Although the original Hebrew version of their work was published during the years 1908-11, there was not a complete English version available until William G. Braude's translation appeared in 1992. Our version of the *Sefer Ha-Aggadah* represents an effort to make this incredible resource accessible to young readers.

This teacher's guide has been written to maximize the usefulness of this book of legends for young readers as an educational resource. Each chapter of the guide is made up of the following components:

1. **Biographies of the Tales' Protagonists**: This section gives a brief biographical sketch of the main characters in each chapter's *aggadot* (plural of *aggadah*). Because all the personalities in this volume are biblical, most will be familiar to you and your students. Nonetheless, this section emphasizes the salient elements of their profiles that apply to the time period mentioned in the stories.

2. **Background for the Teacher**: In this section, the time frames of the stories are placed in the larger context of the biblical narrative. Where appropriate, comments are made regarding any common thematic elements that connect the stories in each chapter.

3. **Motivational Action or Starter**: These are suggestions for introducing the legends by focusing on a key concept or message found in them.

4. **Classroom Discussion**: This section includes questions to stimulate class discussion. Approach them as suggestions. Use them as is or alter them to suit your needs and the needs of your students. Use as many as you want and feel free to add your own.

5. **Classroom Activities**: This section of the teacher's guide suggests activities to enhance your lessons and to make the stories in the text more relevant to the students' lives.

6. **Family Discussion Activities**: This section is included to foster Jewish education in the home. There are several suggestions from which you can choose.

7. **Answer Key**: These answers are provided for the *Activity Book for Sefer Ha-Aggadah: The Book of Legends for Young Readers*.

It is my hope that this teacher's guide will serve you well, as you explore with your students *Sefer Ha-Aggadah: The Book of Legends for Young Readers*.

Behatzlachah!

Ellen Singer

1 • LIGHT AND FIRE

BIOGRAPHIES OF THE TALES' PROTAGONISTS

As described in the Torah, Adam and Eve, Noah, and the people of the Tower of Babel are the earliest ancestors of human beings. They are our first models for dealing with God, our earth, and each other. While Noah is identified as worthy of being saved from the Flood because he "walked with God," all these characters show us that we are as likely to stumble as we proceed down the path of life as we are to walk unerringly.

BACKGROUND FOR THE TEACHER

The three stories in this chapter are etiological, meaning that they seek to explain the origins of particular phenomena. "Light and Fire" offers not only explanations about the creation of human beings but also the sources of animal names, the reason we die, and the background behind the origins of fire. "Noah and the Lie" describes how the Lie and Wickedness survived the Flood that was intended to wipe out all evil. And "The Tower of Babel" recounts how the peoples of the world, who up to this point lived in one small area and spoke one language, came to be scattered throughout the world and to speak many different languages. These are not explanations that we have to take literally. Rather we learn from them that ancient peoples, just like people today, sought to order their lives by providing answers to some very basic life questions.

These stories emerge from sections of the beginning chapters of *Bereshit*/Genesis, the first book of the Torah. They are wholly or partially familiar to your students. The challenge in presenting them is to guide students to delve below the surface to find new meanings and thought-provoking ideas.

MOTIVATIONAL ACTION OR STARTER
(Choose one of the following before reading the chapter.)

1. Fire—At the top of the chalkboard, make a chart with the heading Fire. Underneath that heading write Positive on one side and Negative on the other. Ask the students to fill in the chart with positive and negative characteristics of fire. After the chart has been completed, tell the students that we are now going to read a story about Adam and Eve. Point out that fire plays an important role in the story. Ask the students to compare the characteristics of the fire in the story with the positive and negative characteristics listed on the chart.

2. Darkness—Ask the students to close their eyes. Then tell the class: "Imagine for a moment that you are a small child in your bed at night. Your room is very dark. Although you strain your eyes, you still cannot see your toys and books all over the room. Then you notice a change occurring. Slowly the clouds blocking the moon begin to float away, and little by little your room begins to fill with the soft light of the moon." Now have the students open their eyes. Ask the students: "How did you feel when the room was totally dark? How did you feel once the moonlight began to fill the room?" Spend a few moments allowing the students to share the sensations they imagined when their eyes were closed.

   Now read the story about Adam and Eve, which includes a description of Adam and Eve's first experience with darkness. Then tell the class: "We are going to examine how their experience compares with the imaginary one you just had."

CLASSROOM DISCUSSION

1. If you began with motivational action 1, ask: "How is fire depicted in our story? Which of the positive and negative characteristics listed on our chart are included (or hinted at) in the story? What Jewish rituals emphasize fire as a gift of God?" [the lighting of Shabbat and holiday candles, *Havdalah* and Chanukah candles]

2. If you began with motivational action 2, ask: "How did Adam and Eve's first experience with darkness compare to your feelings during the introductory exercise? Is the greatest fear of darkness not being able to see well? How can fire ease that fear? What hint does the story give that fire is not necessarily all good?"

3. More questions for discussion:

    a. Adam named the animals. Ask: "Why do you think God gave Adam this task instead of naming them and telling Adam, 'This is a cow, this is a peacock, this is a tiger'? How important is naming? If you could change the name of one animal, which one would it be? What new name would you give it? Who gave you your name? Do you know why? If you were named after someone, do you know anything about that person?"

    b. We usually think of the pairs on Noah's ark as pairs of animals. The story "Noah and the Lie" implies that ideas or concepts were also paired. The Lie tries to pair up with others, but he is rejected until he finds a willing partner in Wickedness. Ask: "Whom do you think Beauty paired with? What about Truth? Can you think of some ideas or concepts and give their pairs?" Here are some more ideas or concepts: jealousy, kindness, anger, humility, and honesty. "Who do you think were their pairs?"

    c. "The Tower of Babel" offers an explanation for the many languages spoken by the people in the world. Ask the students: "How many different languages do you speak? Have you ever visited a place where English was not the main language spoken?" (It is not necessary for the students to have traveled to a foreign country; there are many ethnic neighborhoods in North America where English is not the primary language.) Ask: "What did this experience feel like? How did you communicate?" Tell the students to imagine themselves in a room with Jews from all over the world. Ask: "Is there a way you might communicate? Is there a common 'language' of Jews and Judaism beyond Hebrew?"

    d. All these stories are about the origins of things or ideas. Ask: "What origins are explained in each story?" List the following on the board: fire; animal names; why we die; why there are lies; why the people of the world speak so many different languages; human beings. Ask the students to identify the story to which they belong.

CLASSROOM ACTIVITIES

1. In the story "Light and Fire," Adam and Eve take comfort in God's gift of fire, which we bless in the *Havdalah* prayer. Divide the class into small groups and have each group write a television commercial about the virtue of *Havdalah* as a Jewish home ritual. Have the class select one of the commercials for presentation at a Friday night service at the temple.

2. In "The Tower of Babel," the workers cared more for the bricks than they cared for one another. Ask the students the meaning of treating a person with dignity. Have the class read newspapers or watch newscasts to find a company that does not treat its workers with dignity. Have the students start a letter-writing campaign to that company by writing their own letters in class and then asking their parents, friends, or relatives to join the campaign.

3. In "Noah and the Lie," Noah allows the Lie to enter the ark after the Lie has found a mate. This story may be telling us that lies are necessary evils with which we must learn to live. Select a few students to role-play scenarios that throw into question the idea that telling the truth is always good. For example, have the students dramatize a situation in which a person must decide whether or not to relay bad news (about a family member who has fallen ill or died) to a relative whose own health is not good. Once the role-play is finished, ask the students: "Is telling the truth always good? Is it worth telling the truth when doing so may wound a person's feelings or even cause physical harm? Under what circumstances may it be appropriate to lie?"

FAMILY DISCUSSION ACTIVITIES

1. Have the students discuss with their parents the names of members of their family. Ask: "Who named whom, and from where do the names come?" Have the students ask each family member: "What animal would you be if you could be any animal? Why? Would you give the animal a new name?"

2. Provide the families with the text for *Havdalah* and a list of the necessary supplies and where to get them. To encourage family *Havdalah* observance, organize a class *Havdalah* service for one Saturday evening. Begin by telling or reading "Light and Fire." Proceed to the *Havdalah* service. You may wish to follow the service with additional storytelling and refreshments.

3. Provide copies of the story "Slander Slays Three" from *The Classic Tales: 4,000 Years of Jewish Lore*, Ellen Frankel (New York: Jason Aronson, Inc., 1989). Have the families discuss the story in connection with "Noah and the Lie."

ANSWER KEY

Activity Book, Chapter 1
Page 1

Adam was the name of the first man. **Eve** was the name of the first women. Their first home was the **Garden** of **Eden**. The **snake** convinced them to make the world's first mistake, and they ate from the **tree**. As a punishment, they had to leave home. After leaving, they were very scared because it started to get **dark**, but they felt better when they saw the **moon** and the **stars**. God called the seventh day **Shabbat** and made it a day of **rest**.

Page 3

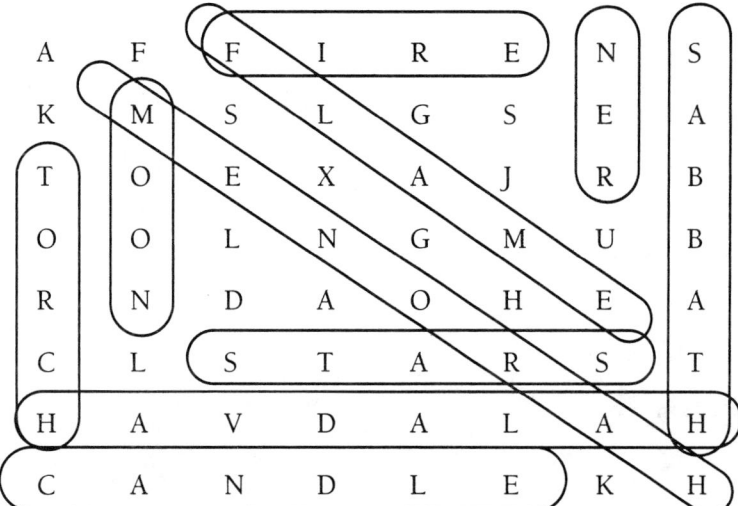

Page 4

Sample pairings could look like this:

2 • HOW SHALL YOU BE BLESSED?

BIOGRAPHIES OF THE TALES' PROTAGONISTS

The stories in this chapter shift their emphasis from the beginnings of the world to the beginnings of the Jewish people. In "How Shall You Be Blessed?" Abraham and Sarah, the first patriarch and matriarch, come into focus as very righteous people, deserving of God's blessing. Their description in this story supports the image found in numerous Torah passages that mention Abraham or Abraham and Sarah. We know they are loyal and full of faith (Gen. 12: God commands them to travel to Canaan; Gen. 22: God puts Abraham to the ultimate test of sacrificing his son). We know they are hospitable by the way they treat the angels disguised as simple travelers (Gen. 18). And we know Abraham is compassionate and wise from the story of Sodom and Gomorrah (Gen. 18-19).

The Torah does not present the patriarchs and matriarchs as perfect and unfailing. They all have faults that make them very real and very human. An example of this is the portrayal of Jacob (the third patriarch) and Esau, the twin sons of Isaac and Rebecca. Even before leaving the womb, the two brothers struggled in a way that foreshadowed their future troubles (Gen. 25). In this chapter, the two selections from the *aggadah* highlight their character differences. These stories also help explain why Jacob, the younger of the two, was ultimately the one to follow in his father's footsteps and inherit the privilege and responsibility of carrying out God's *berit*, "covenant," with the Jewish people.

BACKGROUND FOR THE TEACHER

All the stories in this chapter express important messages about how we are to live our lives. Although the messages are not identical, they do overlap. In "How Shall You Be Blessed?" we are reminded of the reciprocal nature of our relationship with God. God recognizes the righteous behavior of Abraham and Sarah and searches for an appropriate acknowledgment. The answer for God is to bless them with future generations who will possess their fine qualities. This is not merely a story about reward, but it is also a comment on the value of one's life. We learn that the worth of our lives is not measured only by what we do in the present but also by what we contribute to the future. For many of us that contribution may be children and grandchildren, but for all of us there is a wide range of ways to act on this ideal.

"Jacob and Esau—Like Two Plants" reminds us that young children, like young plants, grow and change. What we will be like as adults can rarely be unequivocally known when we are young. We all need to be nurtured so that we will grow to our fullest potential and develop in positive ways.

The last story in this chapter, "The Bargain," builds on the Torah stories that describe the bargaining and trickery between Jacob and Esau. In this selection from the *aggadah*, Jacob demonstrates his clever nature, as well as his understanding that all we have is really on loan from God.

MOTIVATIONAL ACTION OR STARTER

Ask the class to define the word *blessing*. Write the responses on the board. Then ask: "If you were going to bless someone, how would you bless that person?" List these responses on the board, too. Introduce "How Shall You Be Blessed?" by telling the students that we are now going to read a story about a blessing to see who is blessed, who is doing the blessing, and if any of our definitions fit the blessing given in the story.

CLASSROOM DISCUSSION

1. Who is doing the blessing in our story? Who is being blessed? How are they being blessed? How does the blessing in the story fit in with our list of definitions of a blessing?

2. More questions for discussion:

   a. God and the angels discuss how to bless Abraham and Sarah. Below are some possible choices:

      1) Make them upright and honest.

      2) Give them love for each other.

      3) Give them wisdom.

      4) Give them descendants who will follow in their footsteps.

      Rank the above in the order of your preferences for blessing. Tell the students to be prepared to explain their response to others.

   b. In "How Shall You Be Blessed?" one of the angels answers God's question by telling a story, a common way of making a point. Ask the students to give an example of a time when they told a story to explain an idea they had.

   c. Review the book *Listen to the Trees*, Molly Cone, UAHC Press, 1995, and choose appropriate material to use in conjunction with the stories in this chapter.

      1) Based on "How Shall You Be Blessed?" and material from *Listen to the Trees*, make a list of those things we get from trees.

      2) If we only take from trees, what will be the consequences? What do we give to trees? What can we give to trees?

      3) What did the man in the angel's story take from the tree? What did he give it?

   d. In "The Bargain," Jacob says to Esau, "Everything belongs to God. Yet God allows me to use these things as I need them." Help the students explore the meaning of this statement.

      1) Have the students make and discuss a list of their possessions. Write the list on the board and, for each item, ask: "If this item is on loan from God, how should you treat it?"

      2) Ask the students: "In light of Jacob's statement, how would you complete the following sentences?"

      I should treat my pet _____.

      I should treat my friends _____.

      I should treat the earth _____.

      I should treat my computers and all my games _____.

CLASSROOM ACTIVITIES

1. In the story "How Shall You Be Blessed?" we learn how God blessed the descendants of Abraham and Sarah because of their goodness. Have the class make a short list of Jewish characters whose traits we should emulate. Divide the class into several groups and assign one character to each group. Have each group draw its character on part of a long sheet of butcher paper (or several pieces of poster board taped together) that has been placed on the floor or taped to the wall.

Encourage each group to draw its picture in such a way that the characters are linked together (e.g., by sharing the same background or by overlapping). Ask the temple rabbi or administrator for an appropriate place to hang the student "mural."

2. Some rabbinic teachings say that Jacob and Esau, as they are described in the story "Jacob and Esau—Like Two Plants," are two sides of the same person. If possible, have several students bring instant cameras to class. Have the students make a list of five personal character traits. Have them take five photos of themselves, each photo dramatizing one trait. After the pictures have been developed, tell the students to assemble the photos on a large sheet of paper (an 11 x17 sheet will do) and write a short essay about themselves and their traits alongside the photos.

3. In "The Bargain," Jacob agrees to Esau's bargain to take "everything God gives." Esau believes that he has outsmarted Jacob, for taking everything that God gives really means giving everything back to God. As Jacob says, "Everything belongs to God." In that same spirit, ask the students to pledge for a certain number of weeks a portion of their allowance to *tzedakah*. Have them decide on the charity to which they will send what they have set aside. Before they turn over their *tzedakah* portion, have them write essays about the concept of "giving back."

FAMILY DISCUSSION ACTIVITIES

1. Provide families with the excerpts from Genesis 25-29 that describe Jacob and Esau. Ask them to explore plant and tree reference books to find the characteristics of myrtle trees and wild roses. Then, using the Genesis excerpts, ask them to discuss the validity of the descriptions of Esau as a wild rose and Jacob as a myrtle tree in "Jacob and Esau—Like Two Plants."

2. After reading "How Shall You Be Blessed?" as a family, ask the parents to make a list of positive traits they believe their parents (i.e., the students' grandparents) passed down to them. At the same time, have the children list positive traits their parents have passed down to them. Then have the parents and the children share the lists. They may choose to send a copy of the story and the lists to the grandparents.

3. Provide copies of the story "The Two Jewels" from *The Classic Tales: 4,000 Years of Jewish Lore*, Ellen Frankel (New York: Jason Aronson, Inc., 1989). Have the families discuss the story in connection with the stories in this chapter.

ANSWER KEY

Activity Book, Chapter 2
Page 6

God wanted to bless Abraham and Sarah, but they already possessed three good qualities: **wisdom**, **honesty**, and **love**. Therefore, to help God decide how to bless them, an **angel** told a story about a **tree** that grew in the wilderness. A wandering man was grateful for its **shade** and blessed it so that it would have good offspring. Using this story as an example, God decided to bless Abraham ansd Sarah with **children** who would be just like their **parents**.

Page 7

1. A
2. D
3. B
4. C

3 • WHAT IS A PROMISE WORTH?

BIOGRAPHIES OF THE TALES' PROTAGONISTS

Joseph, Jacob's favorite child and the first child of Jacob's beloved wife Rachel, incurred the wrath of his siblings. As a result, he was sold to caravan traders and taken to Egypt. Once in Egypt he was sold to Potiphar, a courtier of Pharaoh and his chief steward (Gen. 37). Joseph's fortunes were going smoothly until the wife of Potiphar grew angry when her attempts to seduce Joseph were unsuccessful. In anger she falsely accused him of licentious behavior, and Joseph ended up in prison (Gen. 39). In "What Is a Promise Worth?" we encounter Joseph while he is still imprisoned and feeling forlorn. He does not recognize that his prison encounters with the Pharaoh's cupbearer and the baker are fortuitous and will contribute to his future release from prison.

BACKGROUND FOR THE TEACHER

The stories in this chapter take us to Egypt, site of Joseph's triumphant rise to power and later the seat of our great affliction. While in prison, Joseph feels abandoned by God. At the beginning of "What Is a Promise Worth?" we find Joseph in prison feeling lonely and uncertain of his future. We quickly learn that God has not forgotten him, and we see that with God's help, he impresses Pharaoh. Finally, with his display of intense loyalty to his father, he teaches Pharaoh the true meaning of a promise.

The two other tales in this chapter also take place in Egypt. But they are set in a time when Joseph is no longer remembered, much less respected. Both stories build on verses from the early chapters of Exodus. In "Pharaoh's Trick" (Exod. 1), we meet the Pharaoh "who did not know Joseph" and who sees the growing Israelite population as a threat. He uses a request for a special favor as a ploy for tricking them into slavery. In "An Egyptian Saved Us" (Exod. 2), we see how an *aggadah* interprets the words of the daughters of Jethro when they describe Moses' defense of them and their sheep by saying "an Egyptian saved us." In this story, Moses cleverly turns around their words and adds a bit of irony as he gives credit to Pharaoh (the enslaver) as the catalyst for their rescue from the aggressive shepherds.

MOTIVATIONAL ACTION OR STARTER

List the following on the board or photocopy for the students:

1. I promised to help my mom or dad with some household chores.
2. I promised not to repeat an embarrassing secret a friend told me.
3. I promised to complete my homework before watching television.
4. I promised to practice my musical instrument without being reminded to do so.
5. I promised to clean up my room.
6. I promised to take care of my family pet.
7. I promised to write thank you notes for birthday presents.
8. I promised to help a neighbor with yard work.
9. I promised to call my grandparent just to talk.
10. I promised to get ready for school on time.

Have the students indicate on a piece of paper which of the above promises they have made recently. Have them place a check next to the promises they have kept. Ask for volunteers to give an example of one promise they kept or broke and why. If no one volunteers, proceed to introduce the story. Tell the class: "From this exercise we see that many of us make promises, some of which we keep and some of which we break. We are now going to read a story about the power of a promise to learn about the importance of keeping promises."

CLASSROOM DISCUSSION

1. What did Joseph promise Pharaoh? What did Joseph promise his father, Jacob? How did Joseph lead Pharaoh to conclude that "a promise is a promise"? What do the above exercise and the message in the story tell us about keeping promises?

2. More questions for discussion:

   a. Why was it so important to Jacob that he be buried in the Holy Land, the Land of Israel?

   b. At the beginning of the story, Joseph wondered if God had forgotten him "the way people forget a broken promise." Ask the class: "Has anyone ever broken a promise made to you? How did you feel? Did you ever break a promise you made to someone else? How did you feel?"

   c. Have those students who are more comfortable expressing themselves in visual terms compare and contrast their visual images of Joseph: first, when he stood before Pharaoh surrounded by priests, astrologers, and magicians ("Joseph felt like the smallest man in the whole room.") and second, when he sat and taught Pharaoh Hebrew.

   d. In "Pharaoh's Trick," Pharaoh deceives his loyal and hard-working subjects, the Children of Israel. Ask: "In your opinion, which is worse—that Pharaoh maneuvered the Children of Israel into slavery or that he asked for a 'special favor' when he really meant something else?"

   e. Pharaoh is the title given the rulers of ancient Egypt. Have the students describe the Pharaoh mentioned in each of these stories. Ask: "In what ways are they similar, and in what ways do they differ?"

   f. In "An Egyptian Saved Us," the words of the women whom Moses defended are interpreted in two ways. Ask the students which of the following statements they think best describes the message behind this story.

      1) Just because Moses was dressed like an Egyptian did not mean that he was one. This story reminds us of the saying that "you should not judge a book by its cover." (You should also not judge people by the way they are dressed.)

      2) Moses was a modest man. Instead of saying, "Yes, I saved you," he says, "Because of other events in my life, I was in the right place at the right time to be able to help you."

CLASSROOM ACTIVITIES

1. In "What Is a Promise Worth?" we learn that Pharaoh wanted to master the Hebrew language, but he was unable to do so. If he had learned Hebrew, he might have been able to save himself and future pharaohs from the grief they brought upon themselves. Your class may have better luck. Designate a day for teaching Hebrew and invite parents to class to join in this teaching experience. This session should show the students how challenging teaching a class actually is.

Emphasize projects that will help the students build up confidence in their teaching ability. Help them plan their lessons. Teaching the *Alef-Bet*, the accompanying vowels, and a few basic words is a great place to start.

2. In "Pharaoh's Trick," we see how Pharaoh tricked the Jews into making an enormous quantity of bricks per day. One way we remember the terrible task of making mortar and bricks during our slavery in Egypt is by eating *charoset* at the Passover seder. Have the students collect family *charoset* recipes and then spend time in the temple kitchen making the different kinds of *charoset*. Ask the students what we learn through the process of remembering.

3. In "An Egyptian Saved Us," we see an example of Moses' humility when he attributed his rescue of the seven women at the well to his exile from Egypt. Have the students bring in newspaper or magazine clippings about heroic deeds done by individuals. Ask: "In each situation, did the person take credit for the deed?" Have the students compare those deeds with heroic deeds performed by Moses at the parting of the Sea of Reeds (Exod. 14-15). Ask the students if Moses took personal credit for what he had done. Divide the class into groups. Have each group make a poster using the clippings that were brought to class, leaving space for a list of traits every hero should have (e.g., humility, bravery, faith in God, etc.).

FAMILY DISCUSSION ACTIVITIES

1. Ask members of the family to make realistic promises to one another. Have them write down the promises, put them in an envelope, and store them in a good place for safekeeping. Have them agree that at a given time (e.g., one week, two months) they will open up the envelope and review what they have written. Have them discuss: "How easy or difficult was it to keep your promises? What did you learn about making promises that you can use in the future?"

2. Ask the families to discuss: "Who saved the daughters of Jethro?" [Some possible answers are Moses, Pharaoh, God.]

3. Ask the students to follow in Joseph's footsteps by teaching Hebrew to an older person. Have them share one recent Hebrew lesson with their parents or make arrangements for the family to study Hebrew together on a regular basis.

4. In "What Is a Promise Worth?" Pharaoh learns a valuable lesson from Joseph, who is (presumably) both younger and less experienced in life. Ask the parents to discuss examples of something they have learned from their children.

ANSWER KEY

Activity Book, Chapter 3
Page 11
Although Joseph had done nothing wrong, he was put in **prison** in Egypt. One day, he was released and asked to interpret the **dreams** of the Egyptian ruler, who was called **Pharaoh**. Joseph was so successful that the **astrologers** and **magicians** in the court grew jealous. They insisted Joseph be **tested** to see if he knew the different languages spoken in Egypt. After Joseph proved he could speak all the languages of Egypt, he tried to teach Pharoah the **Hebrew** language. After Pharaoh found that language too difficult, he made Joseph promise not to tell anyone.

Page 13

"Are you able to understand me?"

Page 14

1. gem
2. get
3. loop
4. lope
5. lot
6. meet
7. met
8. mop
9. mope
10. mote
11. peel
12. pet
13. poem
14. pole
15. pool
16. pop
17. pot
18. tell
19. temple
20. top

Page 15

4 • LOVING THE SMALL THINGS

BIOGRAPHIES OF THE TALES' PROTAGONISTS

Moses is the best known of all biblical personalities. This is probably because of the high drama of his story as detailed in the Torah and his central role in leading and molding the Jewish people. (The annual television airing of the movie *The Ten Commandments* has also indelibly imprinted a certain image of Moses in the minds of many of our students.)

We learn that Moses, from the very beginning of his life, was chosen for a special purpose. He was not only saved from the terrible decree that called for the death of all Hebrew baby boys, but he was also given shelter in the palace of the pharaoh who made the decree (Exod. 2). The Torah then fast forwards to the adult Moses, whose murderous response to the injustice of an Egyptian slave master forced him to flee to the wilderness. In the wilderness, his kindness to the daughters of Jethro, the Midianite priest, led to an invitation to join Jethro's household. He married Zipporah, one of Jethro's daughters, and they had a son, Gershom (Exod. 2).

At this point Moses' life took a dramatic turn. While tending his father-in-law's flock, he encountered an angel of God in a blazing fire out of a bush. Awestruck, Moses reacted hesitantly to God's call to leadership. He modestly questioned God, "Who am I that I should go to Pharaoh and free the Israelites from Egypt?" And God responded, "I will be with you, and it shall be your sign that it was I who sent you." Moses demurred further but was finally swayed by both God's miracles and reassurances. Together with his brother, Aaron, Moses convinced the elders of the Israelites of his God-given mission (Exod. 3, 4). From there, Moses began the long journey toward redemption of the Israelite slaves. This journey, punctuated by the ten plagues (Exod. 7-11), culminated in the miracle at the Sea of Reeds (Exod. 14).

BACKGROUND FOR THE TEACHER

God's relationship with and responsibility for the Jewish people is an underlying theme in the stories in this chapter. In "Loving the Small Things," God tests Moses to see if he is suitable to care for "even the smallest baby among My flock, the Israelites." In "The Burning Bush," God explains that like the bush burning with fire but not destroyed, so, too, "My people cannot be destroyed" despite the burn of hard labor. In the same story God also stresses the divine will to protect the Jewish people by telling Moses, "To save My people Israel, I need your love and not your fear."

Finally, in "Matzah—The Small Miracle," God responds to Moses' fears that once the Israelites are freed, he will not know how to care for them. God reassures Moses. "Place your trust in Me, Moses… you will see how I care for My people." This sense of responsibility on God's part is an important foundation of Jewish thought, as is the concept of our reciprocal relationship with God.

MOTIVATIONAL ACTION OR STARTER
(Choose one of the following before reading the chapter.)

1. Ask the students: "What does a shepherd do? What is the difference between a good shepherd and a bad one? How would a responsible shepherd act? How would an irresponsible shepherd act?" Tell the students that, in the first story in this chapter, we are going to explore how Moses measures up to his role as a shepherd.

2. Ask the students: "If you were given the task of looking for God, where would you look?" (If some students respond that they do not believe in God, ask them to suspend their disbelief for a moment and address this question.) List their responses on the board. Then ask: "Where did Moses first encounter God?" [The burning bush is the appropriate response.] Tell the class that we are now going to read the story of Moses' first encounter with God, paying attention to God's choice of location and the reason for it.

CLASSROOM DISCUSSION

1. If you began with motivational action 1, ask: "What kind of shepherd was Moses? How did he meet his responsibilities? What kind of shepherd is God? How do Moses and God compare in this role?"

2. If you began with motivational action 2, ask: "Where did Moses first encounter God? Why did God choose to speak out of a thorn bush?" Have the students look at the list of the places we indicated we would look for God. Ask: "How do the places on our list compare to the thorn bush?"

3. More questions for discussion:

    a. Moses was responsible for caring for Jethro's flock. God is responsible for caring for the Jewish people. Ask the students: "Have you ever been responsible for anyone or anything? A pet? A younger brother, a sister, a cousin, or a friend? Have you ever been responsible for taking care of someone who is sick? How did you fulfill your responsibilities in these cases?"

    b. Have the students role-play a variety of trees, those mentioned in the story and additional ones for which you should provide pictures. In their roles as trees, have the students state their case as to why God should choose them to speak to Moses. (Students may refer to the story for some help, but they should be encouraged to be creative and come up with additional ideas not given in "Loving the Small Things.") Also have one student play the role of God.

    c. When the trees asked God why the Holy One chose to speak to Moses from the thorn bush, God replies, "To show that God is everywhere on the earth, even in the lowly thorn bush." Have the class give other examples of unlikely places where we might sense (or seek) God's presence.

    d. The third story refers to matzah as a small miracle. Ask the students to make a list of Small Miracles and/or Big Miracles. Have them share their lists. Then ask: "What is miraculous about matzah? What is the difference between a small and a big miracle? Which of the following is a small miracle and which is a big miracle: the rising and setting of the sun, the blooming of a flower, a rainbow, the birth of a litter of puppies or kittens, the splitting of the Sea of Reeds, the birth of the State of Israel, surviving an earthquake?" (Add other items.)

    e. Write the following words on the board: kindness, humbleness, love, fear, trust, responsibility. Point out that the stories in the chapter express all these basic human traits. Have the class reread the stories and match the above traits with the appropriate story. (In some cases, a trait may be found in more than one story.) [Possible suggestions include: "Loving the Small Things"—kindness, responsibility, humbleness; "The Burning Bush"—fear, love; "Matzah—The Small Miracle"—responsibility, trust.]

CLASSROOM ACTIVITIES

1. The story "Loving the Small Things" emphasizes that even small and quiet things receive attention from God and others. Have students role-play scenarios in which being small and quiet may

be better than being big and loud: Select several students to dramatize a situation in which one person asks favors from another (e.g., to borrow a bike or a set of roller blades, to help with homework, or to share an after-school treat). At first have the students ask one another for one or more of these favors in a loud and demanding voice. Then have them ask for the same favors in a kind, gentle voice. Ask the students: "Which voice works? Why? In what situations is one voice more effective than another?" Have them determine which voice works better in an emergency such as a fire. Ask: "Would whispering help in such a situation?" Explain to the students that different tones of expression are required for different circumstances and that sometimes being quiet and small is much more effective than being loud and big.

2. In "Loving the Small Things," we see that the thorn bush was plain and simple compared to the fig and carob trees. Ask the students to make a list of plain but useful objects and compare these objects with complicated and fancy ones. (You may have to brainstorm with the whole class on which objects fall into which category.) Ask the students which object is better at fulfilling its purpose. Have the students interview their parents about these two types of objects. Brainstorm with the students some questions they might ask their parents: "Have fancy cars broken down more often than plainer ones? Are kitchen utensils like blenders, coffee makers, and automatic can openers always better or more efficient than simpler tools?"

3. The story "Matzah—The Small Miracle" teaches us that the Children of Israel in the wilderness were truly blessed to receive matzah and manna from God. Today we rely on people who perform deeds of loving-kindness to make sure people do not go hungry. Have your students organize a food pantry at their temple. If one already exists, have them spend some class time working in it. Contact a local food distributor and have the students help collect or distribute food. If the students live in an urban area where there are shelters for the homeless, have them spend time in the temple kitchen making sandwiches and packages that they can deliver as a class to a shelter. (Be sure to contact the shelter's administrator first.)

FAMILY DISCUSSION ACTIVITIES

1. Ask the families to discuss the soothing voice of Moses' father used by God in "The Burning Bush." Have the family members describe voices that soothe and calm them. Have them discuss the difference between loving God and fearing God and the difference between loving and fearing a parent or loving and fearing God.

2. Another family discussion topic: By the end of Pesach we often tire of the taste of matzah. Ask: "How does the story 'Matzah—The Small Miracle' change how you feel about matzah? If, like the Children of Israel, you could make a food that would sustain you for thirty days, what would it be? Why?"

ANSWER KEY

Activity Book, Chapter 4
Page 16

God was impressed with how much Moses cared about small things and decided to speak to Moses from a tree. At first all the trees and bushes wanted God to speak from them. The **fig** tree thought God should speak to Moses from it because it provided Moses with **water** from its roots when he wandered thorugh the **wilderness**. The **carob** tree argued that it shoud speak to Moses because it was used in the flour for the **bread** at Moses' marriage feast. But God chose the **thorn bush** to show that even something that does not seem important is valuable in God's eye's.

5 • A TIME TO PRAY, A TIME TO ACT

BIOGRAPHIES OF THE TALES' PROTAGONISTS

Moses, like the patriarchs, Abraham, Isaac, and Jacob, was imperfect. He was not necessarily a "born leader." In fact, when God approached Moses through the burning bush and called on him to lead the Children of Israel, Moses questioned the wisdom of God's choice. Moses doubted his own ability to sway either the Children of Israel or Pharaoh. He was quick to point out that as a stutterer he would not make a very good spokesman. But God assured Moses, and finally he agreed (Exod. 3-4).

Moses executed his duties well, as he stated his case before Pharaoh and as he prepared the Israelites for the rushed departure from Egypt. By the time Moses and the Jews reached the Sea of Reeds, Moses had accumulated experience as a leader and a spokesman. Yet, in "A Time to Pray, A Time to Act," Moses seems to be still evolving as a leader. He appears to freeze at the Sea of Reeds with the Egyptians fast approaching (Exod. 14). Even the brave, assertive response of Nahshon does not immediately spur him to action. Only when God insists, does Moses finally respond in an effective leadership fashion.

BACKGROUND FOR THE TEACHER

Moses, Pharaoh, and the Children of Israel all play central roles in the three stories in this chapter. But the primary role is occupied by God, as the shaper of our destiny when we leave Egypt and begin our experience in the wilderness. In these stories, God is characterized as both an external force and an internal one. In "A Time to Pray, A Time to Act," a divine inner strength moves Nahshon in his conviction that the only response to the situation is action. Moses, on the other hand, looks outside himself for divine guidance.

In "The Horses of the Egyptians," a mighty Pharaoh finally comes to comprehend the power of God. The external signs of God's might displayed at the Sea of Reeds, as well as the internal change of Pharaoh's heart, lead Pharaoh to conclude that his might is no match for that of God.

Finally, in "Gathering Manna," we encounter God as the source of our sustenance and as the parent who expects acknowledgment. While both of these focus on God as an external force, they are aimed at moving us to turn inward to God. This story concludes with the challenge for us to find ways to turn our hearts to God every day.

MOTIVATIONAL ACTION OR STARTER

Write on the board Times to Pray and Times to Act. Have the students offer suggestions for filling in the two columns. Tell the students that we are now going to read a story about Moses and the Children of Israel at the Sea of Reeds, paying particular attention to how Moses responds to the situation.

CLASSROOM DISCUSSION

1. How did Moses respond to the situation at the Sea of Reeds? Which did he choose, prayer or action? Can prayer be a form of taking action? Why? Why not?

2. More questions for discussion:

a. Nahshon, a man from the tribe of Judah, called on his fellow Jews to stop bickering and act. Ask: "Which title do you think best fits him: man of action, hero, man of faith, or reckless fool? Why?"

b. Why do you think the people did not follow Nahshon until Moses called out, "Go forward!"? What does this tell us about how the people viewed Moses? What does this tell us about how the people viewed Nahshon?

c. "The Horses of the Egyptians" concludes with the words "Pharaoh at last understood the power of God." Ask: "Which of the following do you think made the biggest impression on Pharaoh: watching the Sea of Reeds split, seeing his chariots swallowed by the sea, or feeling his heart soften?"

d. Every year at the Passover seder, we read from the hagaddah: *Bechol dor vador chayav adam lirot et atzmo keilu hu yatza mimitzrayim*, "In every generation, each person is obligated to see himself/herself as personally redeemed from Egypt." Have the students, keeping this obligation in mind, write a description of the scene at the Sea of Reeds, as if they were there. [Suggestions: How did you feel about the bickering among the tribes? What did you think when Nahshon entered the water? What was your opinion of Moses' handling of the situation?]

e. When God gave manna (except on Shabbat) to the Jewish people, they were thankful to receive food in the wilderness. We may no longer live in the wilderness, but there are plenty of foods for which we are thankful. Have the class make a list of some of these foods and write a prayer of thankfulness for one or two of them.

CLASSROOM ACTIVITIES

1. In "A Time to Pray, A Time to Act," we are taught the importance of prayer *and* action. Bring *siddurim* to class and, together with the students, examine *bakashot*, which are special prayers of request contained within the text of our main prayers like the *Amidah*. *Bakashot* also thank God for many such qualities as wisdom, forgiveness, health, justice, and peace. Divide the class into small groups and suggest to each group ways to express those prayers in new forms. One group may express the meaning of a *bakashah* in the form of a small dance piece or through a series of tableaux. Another group may use the general ideas expressed in a prayer for justice, freedom, or peace to write a new version of the blessing that relates directly to world events. (Suggest that the students may consult the newspapers or magazines for ideas.) At your religious school service, have the students demonstrate these new prayers.

2. The events described in "A Time to Pray, A Time to Act" are very dramatic. To convey that sense of drama, have the students create a radio or video on-the-scene description of the parting of the Sea of Reeds. Appoint students to write, direct, act, make costumes, and produce sound effects. Have them interview the different characters and play back the interviews for another class. Suggest that they focus on the relationship between Moses and Nahshon.

3. Biblical poetry exists in our prayer book in the form of the song *Mi Chamochah*, which is from the Song at the Sea in Exodus 15. This poem thanks God for the miracle of the parting of the Sea of Reeds. Ask the students: "To what other miracles in our lives may we respond with poetry?" (Examples may include the birth of a brother, sister, or cousin; the recovery of a friend, relative, or personal hero from illness or surgery; an act of *tzedakah* by another.) Have the students, individually or as a class, choose from among these subjects (or others) to compose a poem. Arrange for poetry reading at religious school services or on a Friday night.

FAMILY DISCUSSION ACTIVITIES

1. Provide the families with copies of Ecclesiastes 3:1-8—which begins "A season is set for everything and a time for every experience under heaven: A time to be born and a time to die..."—for reading and discussion. Encourage them to write additional verses using the same format.

2. Have the families imagine that they are among the Children of Israel in the wilderness. Ask: "How would you assign the task of gathering the manna? Who would do it and how often?" (This discussion can be used as a jumping-off point for talking about how family household tasks are delegated and carried out.)

3. Ask the families to discuss: God gave us manna each day (except on Shabbat) to teach us that we must turn our hearts to God every day. Ask them which of the following they think qualifies as turning one's heart to God: praying, picking up litter, doing homework on time, discussing the day's events with one another, helping an elderly person, phoning grandparents, visiting sick people in the hospital, going to Hebrew school, keeping kosher, returning a lost wallet. (Encourage family members to add to the list.)

ANSWER KEY

Activity Book, Chapter 5
Page 21

After the **ten** plagues, Pharaoh decided to let the Children of Israel go free. But then he changed his mind. He and his soldiers got into their **chariots** to chase after the Israelites. They trapped the Israelites at the **Sea** of **Reeds**. When the Israelites grew frightened, Moses began to **pray**. But no one moved except for **Nahshon**, who was from the tribe of **Judah**. Because he had faith that God would help, he walked into the sea up to his **nose**. Finally the sea split, and the Children of Israel walked across on **dry** land.

Page 23

Nahshon of Judah

6 • GOD'S MARVELOUS VOICE

BIOGRAPHIES OF THE TALES' PROTAGONISTS

In this chapter, Moses, our greatest and most revered leader, is once again the main character of the stories. We are reminded how at Mount Sinai Moses proved the strength of his leadership. He not only survived his encounter with the Divine Spirit but also managed to convey to the Children of Israel the message given to him.

Nonetheless, the *aggadah* reminds us that Moses is mortal and God is divine. Faced with the commandment to create a menorah, Moses is uncertain about his ability to comply. God responds readily, as if anticipating Moses' questions before they are asked. Furthermore, at the sight of the golden calf (Exod. 32), Moses again shows such human reactions as anger, impatience, and disappointment. Although disheartened by the lack of faith of the Children of Israel, God ultimately commands Moses to prepare a second set of tablets to replace the first. And Moses, the wise leader, turns his anger that had resulted in the breaking of the first tablets into a lesson about the sanctity of *all* of God's creation.

BACKGROUND FOR THE TEACHER

The experience at Mount Sinai was an extremely dramatic and moving event as described in both the Torah (Exod. 19) and the stories in this chapter. The Children of Israel experienced this awesome occurrence through all their senses. To hear the thunder, to see the lightning, to smell the smoke, to feel the heat, and to taste the acrid smoke-filled air was totally wondrous. This encounter with the Divine was so powerful that it transformed the Children of Israel from a confederation of loosely tied tribes into a united people.

The story "God's Marvelous Voice" focuses on the progress into peoplehood that resulted from the event at Mount Sinai. It is a story that emphasizes the intensity of the moment. The next story "The Menorah" also includes its share of fantastic description, detailing the creation of the *menorah*, but concludes with the quietly reassuring image of the "eternal light" as a symbol of God's omnipresence. Finally, in "The Tablets of the Ten Commandments," we are reminded of Moses' flash of anger upon seeing the golden calf. However, rather than focusing on Moses' anger, the story concludes with the lesson taught by Moses that all things, and by inference all people, are holy.

MOTIVATIONAL ACTION OR STARTER

Ask the students to name the five senses. [sight, hearing, touch/feel, smell, taste] Then ask for examples of how we use them in our everyday lives. Tell the students that we are now going to read a story about the Children of Israel's experience at Mount Sinai, paying special attention to the use of our senses at this momentous event.

CLASSROOM DISCUSSION

1. Have the class examine the list of the five senses and describe how the Children of Israel used them during their experience at Mount Sinai. [Possible answers include: seeing the flames and lightning; hearing the *shofar*, thunder, and God's voice; feeling the heat of the fire; smelling and tasting the air filled with smoke.]

2. More questions for discussion:

   a. "God's Marvelous Voice" asks the question: "What happened to the Children of Israel at Sinai that transformed them from a ragtag collection of twelve tribes into one people?" Ask the students: "What is your answer to this question? How did the rabbis answer this question?"

   b. In "God's Marvelous Voice," Rabbi Yose is quoted as saying that the manna tasted different to each person. Another *midrash* states that the manna tasted like whatever a person wanted it to taste like. Ask: "If you had been there, what do you think the manna would have tasted like?"

   c. "God's Marvelous Voice" concludes: "In speaking to the Children of Israel, God spoke to all the peoples of the world, speaking so every person in every land could hear the word of God." Ask the students which of the statements below they think best explains the meaning of these words and have them give their reasons.

      1) God gave the Torah to all the people of the world, not only to the Jews.

      2) Any person who wants to live as a Jew can, although the person was not born a Jew.

      3) The lessons of the Torah are meaningful for all people, Jews and non-Jews.

   d. Have the students draw their own interpretation of the *menorah* described in "The Menorah."

   e. After the students have read "The Menorah," have them look at (or picture in their minds) the *ner tamid*, the "eternal light," in the sanctuary of their temple. Ask: "What does this light make you think about? Do you look at it differently after reading this story? Why? Why not?"

   f. "The Tablets of the Ten Commandments" concludes: "In this way, Moses showed that everything God created is holy—not only those things that are whole, but even those things that to us seem shattered." Have the students pick one slip of paper from a box being passed around the room. Tell them to decide if what is written on the paper applies to the words of the story. (Examples of what to write on the slips of paper include: a blind person, a mentally disabled person, an old dishwasher, a tree struck by lightning, a banana peel, a toy wagon missing a wheel, a person who lost an arm or leg during a war, a flat tire, a faded family photograph, an empty shoe box.)

   g. Fire is mentioned in each of the stories of this chapter. Have the class compare and contrast the following fire images mentioned: the fire at Mount Sinai, the fire of the *menorah*, and Moses' anger that flared in him like a flame.

CLASSROOM ACTIVITIES

1. In "God's Marvelous Voice," we read how the "Children of Israel heard the sound of the *shofar*" calling them to the foot of Mount Sinai. Use the following exercise to convey to the students the importance of listening to the *shofar*: First blindfold the students. Then silently select five students to blow a *shofar*. (You or someone from the temple may have to demonstrate.) Have the remaining students describe the sound of each *shofar* blast. Ask: "Does the *shofar* blast sound confident, timid, funny, or strong?" Remove the blindfolds from the students, making it possible for them to identify the blower with the sound produced from the *shofar*. Ask: "Did your description of the sound correspond to the person making the sound?" If any of the students are surprised that a particular person produced the sound they heard, explain that sometimes a little person can make a big sound on the *shofar* and a big person a small sound.

2. In "The Menorah," we read how God appointed a specific artist, Bezalel, to design the *menorah*. Tell the students that they are now going to design a pounded-copper image of a Jewish symbol, using a square-foot sheet of copper, nails, and a hammer. Allow them to design a Jewish symbol of their choice (e.g., a *menorah*, their Hebrew name, a Star of David, etc.). Consult with your art teacher in planning this activity.

3. In the story "The Tablets of the Ten Commandments," we learn that even broken objects can be valuable. To convey this sense of value, ask the students to participate in the game of "show and tell." Have them bring in "flawed" or imperfect objects (e.g., a stuffed animal with a missing eye, a repaired cup or dish of great sentimental value, etc.). Ask the students: "Why are these objects still special to you despite their flaws? How may the value of these flawed objects be applied more generally to your lives? Did you ever appreciate something more after you were sick? Did a family member recently have an illness that helped you appreciate that person more?" After "show and tell," have the class discuss other reasons Moses gathered together the pieces of the shattered tablets.

FAMILY DISCUSSION ACTIVITIES

1. Ask the families to discuss the effect of one's tone of voice on a situation. In "God's Marvelous Voice," the voice of God is described as thundering throughout the world. Ask: "In your family, what tone of voice works best? If someone yells, does everyone listen? What happens if someone speaks softly?"

2. Have the families explore the following: The first story in this chapter tells us that "wisdom was in the voice of God, and the voice of God was everywhere at once." If wisdom is everywhere, it therefore follows that we each have at least a little wisdom inside of us. Have the family members describe one or more things they have learned from one another.

ANSWER KEY

Activity Book, Chapter 6
Page 26

The sound of the **shofar** called the Israelites to gather at the foot of Mount **Sinai**. The mountain sparked and shuddered, and Moses spoke to **God**, who responded in a voice that was heard in the **north**, the **south**, the **east**, and the **west**. The voice was like **seven** voices that combined to become all the **languages** spoken on earth. Thus, all who heard understood.

Page 27
Stop 1: Egypt
Stop 2: Sea of Reeds
Stop 3: Mount Sinai
Stop 4: Wilderness
Stop 5: Israel

Page 29
1: I AM ADONAI
2: DO NOT HAVE ANY OTHER GODS
3: DO NOT TAKE GOD'S NAME IN VAIN
4: REMEMBER THE SABBATH
5: HONOR YOUR FATHER AND MOTHER

7 • SHALL THERE BE ONE LAW FOR MAN AND ANOTHER FOR WOMAN?

BIOGRAPHIES OF THE TALES' PROTAGONISTS

The stories in this chapter mention two biblical heroes, Aaron and Joshua, in addition to Moses. Both of these men were closely linked to Moses. The first was his brother, and the second was his successor. All three men occupied positions of leadership.

In Numbers 27, we are introduced to five women, whose names are certainly not as familiar as those of Moses, Aaron, and Joshua but whose actions were heroic in their own way. These five women, Mahlah, Noah, Hoglah, Milcah, and Tirzah, the daughters of Zelophehad, sought redress for an injustice they encountered in the inheritance laws. While their initial motivation may have been to resolve the matter in their favor, their courageous decision to speak out led to a judgment that benefited all future generations of Israelites, both women and men.

BACKGROUND FOR THE TEACHER

To varying degrees the stories in this chapter deal with leadership. In "Shall There Be One Law for Man and Another for Woman?" the daughters of Zelophehad take the lead in calling attention to an injustice in the laws of inheritance. In Numbers 26, God had commanded Moses to take a census of the whole Israelite community. The figures were compiled according to tribal divisions and the clans within each of the tribes. Upon the completion of the census, God further commanded that shares of the land, upon the Israelites' return to the Land of Israel, would be apportioned according to these census figures.

Enter the daughters of Zelophehad (Num. 27), who pointed out that because their father was dead and they were unmarried, they were unfairly excluded from receiving a portion of the land. Until Mahlah, Noah, Hoglah, Milcah, and Tirzah spoke up, the practice of the times dictated that land was inherited only through the male line. Lacking a male line, these women faced forced homelessness. They went to the authorities and insisted they be given "a portion of the land as you have given it to other families." Through their willingness to come forward, we learn the importance of speaking up to redress a wrong and how to achieve our goals effectively. They did not simply demand justice but pointed to the teachings of Moses to support their position: "God is good to all, and God's mercy is for all of Creation, not just for men, but for women, too." It must also be noted that the resolution of the problem underscored the value of equal justice for all Israel. This was most remarkable for the ancient world.

In the second brief story, "Aaron Brings Peace," we see how Aaron used his leadership skills in a quiet behind-the-scenes fashion to reconcile friends who had grown apart. Although Aaron's leadership style differed from that of Moses, Aaron was still quite effective in his own way and deeply loved by his people.

Finally, the last story, "In the Days of the Judges," stresses the importance not only of good leaders but also of loyal subjects. As the story relates, the time of the judges (between the conquest led by Joshua and the period of the kings, beginning with Saul) was an era of much turmoil. The commitment of the Jewish people continuously fell short. Both the king in the rabbis' story and God despair over the inconsistency of their flocks. This is a problem that continues to challenge leaders, great and small, to this day.

MOTIVATIONAL ACTION OR STARTER

(Choose one of the following before reading the chapter.)

1. Ask the students to brainstorm important leadership skills. List these skills on the board. (If the students need help filling out the list, you may offer the following suggestions: wisdom, patience, kindness, compassion, decisiveness.) Once the list is complete, ask the students to copy the list in the order of importance and name leaders, living or dead, who possessed at least some of these qualities.

    Tell the students that we are now going to read a story about how the leaders of some communities dealt with a problem, and we shall see if they displayed any of the leadership qualities we have listed on the board.

2. Ask the students what combinations of people make up a family. List their answers on the board. Tell the students that we are now going to read a story in which five of the characters refer to themselves as a family. Ask: "Do you think they make up a family?"

CLASSROOM DISCUSSION

1. Ask: "Who are the leaders mentioned in 'Shall There Be One Law for Man and Another for Woman?'" [Possible answers include: the daughters of Zelophehad; the local judge; the judges of ten, fifties, hundreds, thousands; the elders; Eleazar the Priest; Moses.] Ask: "Which, if any, of the leadership qualities we listed on the board did they possess?"

2. The five sisters said to the authorities, "Give us a portion of the land as you have given it to other families." Ask: "Do you think they were correct in calling themselves a family? Do you define *family* differently after reading this story? If so, in what ways?"

3. More questions for discussion:

    a. The daughters of Zelophehad took their complaint to the local judge, who in turn referred it to the next highest authority. He in turn referred it to the next highest. This went on and on until Moses was consulted, and he turned to God. Ask: "In your opinion, which of the following two statements best describes the underlying behavior of the community leaders: (1) the community leaders were unwilling to take responsibility for making a judgment on this case; (2) the community leaders were very humble and, recognizing the importance of this decision, did not feel worthy of making a final judgment?" (Set up a debate between students, taking the two different positions.)

    b. Reread the reason given for the judgment in favor of Mahlah, Noah, Hoglah, Milcah, and Tirzah. Ask: "What is it? Who else may have been affected by the outcome of this judgment?"

    c. In "Aaron Brings Peace," we read that Aaron knew how "to seek peace, and he knew how to love peace." Ask the students: "What is the difference between seeking peace and loving peace? Can you seek peace without loving it? Can you love peace without seeking it?"

    d. According to the story, Aaron set the wheels in motion for the two friends to make up. Ask: "Does it matter that Aaron was somewhat deceptive in arranging the reunion of the two friends? Are there times when a slight deception is acceptable for a good cause?"

    e. At the end of "In the Days of the Judges," God says, "What shall I do with My children? All I wish is that they remember Me and follow the laws of My Torah!" Ask the students: "What should God do with us?"

CLASSROOM ACTIVITIES

1. The lesson we learn from the story "Shall There Be One Law for Man and Another for Woman?" has many applications in modern times. One important application is the celebration of bat mitzvah for women. To explore this change in religious practice, have one group of students find out who were the first women to celebrate their bat mitzvah in the temple. Appoint another group of students to act as journalists and write a description of what these celebrations were like. (Students may search through the temple's archives for photos or interview those *banot mitzvah*.) Have the students send these stories to the temple bulletin.

2. Aaron is given credit for being a peacemaker in the story "Aaron Brings Peace." Ask the students: "Who are the peacemakers in Israel today? Who stands in the way of peace? Why?" Bring in newspaper articles on issues of dispute in Israel to review with the students. Divide the class into two groups, taking opposing positions on the peace process in Israel. Appoint several students as mediators, assigning them the task of helping the two sides settle their dispute.

3. As the king in the story "In the Days of the Judges" provided for his subjects, we, too, can beautify our temples. With the students (in consultation with the synagogue administrator), plan ways in which the class can beautify the synagogue environment. For example, students may plant flowers outside the temple or make potted plants for the temple office staff as an expression of appreciation.

FAMILY DISCUSSION ACTIVITIES

1. Ask the families to discuss the example set by the daughters of Zelophehad as they lead the way in seeking justice not only for themselves but for women of future generations. Suggest that the families explore others in history who have done the same (e.g., Theodor Herzl, Golda Meir, Ghandi, Susan B. Anthony, Clara Barton, Martin Luther King, Hannah Senesh, Abraham Lincoln). Have the parents and children share their knowledge of the accomplishments of these and other courageous leaders or use their home resources to look up information on them.

2. Ask the parents and children to discuss those to whom they turn when faced with difficult decisions.

3. Remind the families that the daughters of Zelophehad refer to themselves as a family. Ask the families to look around at other families they know. Ask: "How many families are made up of a mom and dad, married for the first time, with children to whom they gave birth? How many are made up of people brought together under different circumstances?" Have the families discuss what they consider defines a family.

4. Have the families discuss how they would deal with a spoiled child. Ask: "Do the Children of Israel, as described in the last story in this chapter, fit the definition of spoiled children?" Have the families brainstorm methods for dealing with spoiled children. Have the students bring the results of this discussion back to class for comparison and contrast.

ANSWER KEY

Activity Book, Chapter 7
Page 31

When Moses divided the land, he gave an equal piece to every **man**. But there were **five** fatherless sisters from the tribe of **Manasseh**, who had no brothers. So these sisters went to their local judge to request their portion of land. But he didn't know how to judge their case—nor did the judges above him. The sisters then went to the priest **Eleazar**, who brought their case to Moses. But even Moses did not know the answer. He went to the **Tent of Meeting** to ask God, and God responded: "**Equal** justice: This is the **law** of Israel."

Page 34

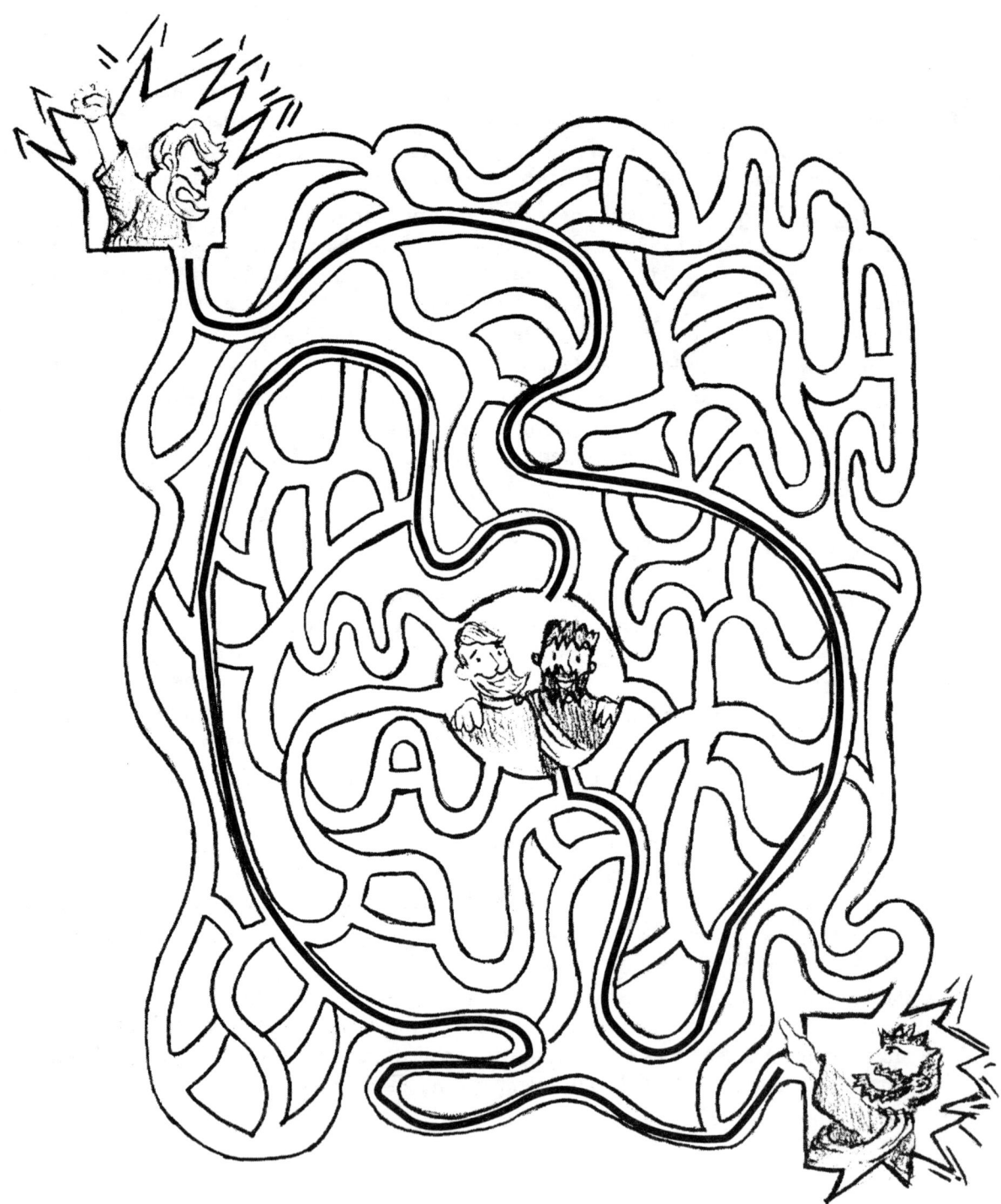

8 • DEBORAH, WOMAN OF LIGHT

BIOGRAPHIES OF THE TALES' PROTAGONISTS

Women play central roles in all three stories in this chapter. Deborah, Naomi, Ruth, and Hannah shine because of their own unique qualities. Deborah is the only woman judge mentioned in the Bible. She was not only wise but also brave. This story highlights her wisdom and helps explain why she was chosen by God for this unique position.

Both Naomi and Ruth are portraits of thoughtfulness, honesty, and piety. When Ruth states her desire to stay with Naomi, Naomi is quick to make certain that Ruth's decision is based on more than a daughter-in-law's devotion. Naomi explicitly spells out the implications of Ruth's choice. To her credit, Ruth does not hesitate in her response, a sign of her sincerity and appreciation of the meaning of her choice.

Finally, Hannah, a devout, childless woman, couching her request in terms of God's plenitude of creatures, asks God for but one child for herself. Her request should not be seen as greedy or excessive. Therefore, her prayers are answered with the birth of an especially blessed son.

BACKGROUND FOR THE TEACHER

Although the women in this chapter are the main protagonists, these stories are not necessarily about women; rather, they are stories about devoted and committed servants of God. Deborah was a judge. The judges, leaders of a single tribe or groups of tribes, were not just legal figures but divinely chosen military leaders, charged with the responsibility of freeing the Israelites from foreign oppression. Deborah is not only the singular woman judge in the Bible, but she is also the only judge who actually judged. (Judges 4:4-5 states: "Deborah, the wife of Lappidoth, was a prophetess; she judged Israel at that time. She used to sit under the palm tree of Deborah, between Ramah and Beth-El in the hill-country of Ephraim, and the Israelites would come to her for decisions.") In "Deborah, Woman of Light," we read that the reward for her commitment to Torah and her concern for others is her appointment as a judge and leader in Israel.

The story of Ruth and Naomi is detailed in *Megillat Rut,* the "Scroll of Ruth," and is traditionally read on Shavuot. Naomi and her husband, Elimelech, and their two sons moved to the country of Moab to escape famine in the Land of Israel. In Moab, Elimelech died. The two sons, who had both married Moabite women, also died, leaving the three women alone. Naomi decided to return to her native land and people and instructed her daughters-in-law, Ruth and Orpah, to remain in their own homeland. Orpah agreed and tearfully stayed in Moab (Ruth 1:14). Ruth, however, insisted on remaining with her mother-in-law, declaring her intention to live as a Jew. Naomi, deeply touched by this show of personal devotion, demanded that Ruth understand the full implications of her choice. Ruth responded in ways that showed her allegiance not only to Naomi but also to God. For her devotion and commitment, Ruth was given a new lease on life—a second husband and children—and her highest reward came posthumously when one of her grandchildren, David, became king of all Israel.

Hannah was a woman in search of the fulfillment of motherhood. She did not just lament her fate and demand that God give her what others also did not have. Instead, joining with other devoted Israelites to honor God at one of the festivals, she implored God to share with her the riches that so many others enjoyed. With her piety, she touched God's heart and was rewarded with a son, who became a great prophet in Israel.

MOTIVATIONAL ACTION OR STARTER

Ask the students to name great women in Jewish history and to give reasons why they consider these women great. Tell the students that we are now going to read stories about several women from the Bible to see if they qualify for a definition of greatness.

CLASSROOM DISCUSSION

1. Have the students read the stories in this chapter. Ask: "Do you think Deborah, Naomi, Ruth, and Hannah were great women of Jewish history? Why? Why not?"

2. More questions for discussion:

    a. Why is it important to Deborah that she create ways for her husband to do good deeds?

    b. Deborah said to herself, "God wants us to study Torah and do good deeds." In the end, God rewards her for caring for others and helping them. Her reward is to make her "light shine for all Israel to see." Ask: "How do you interpret the meaning of her reward?"

    c. Light is a key element in the story "Deborah, Woman of Light." Here are four different references to light: (1) Scholars will study by your *light*; (2) I will call you woman of *light*; (3) I will make your *light* shine for all Israel to see; and (4) a holy spirit (a holy *light*) will shine forth from any one of them who does good deeds. Ask: "What does the reference to *light* in each of these references mean to you?"

    d. Naomi is quick to make sure that Ruth knows that converting to Judaism is a serious move with significant obligations and responsibilities. Have the students list in the order of importance the elements that constitute being a Jew, as detailed by Naomi. (Number one is the most important, number two is the second most important, and so on.) After you have completed your own order, come to agreement with the class as to the best order, e.g., (1) worshiping as a Jew; (2) creating a Jewish home; (3) showing a commitment to the Jewish people; and (4) performing Jewish rituals.

    e. Tell the class to examine Deborah's, Ruth's, and Hannah's rewards for their devotion and commitment. Ask: "In each case, do you think the deeds merit the reward? Do you think the women were properly rewarded?"

CLASSROOM ACTIVITIES

1. Candles play an important part in the story "Deborah, Woman of Light." Candles are especially important in Judaism because they are used to sanctify Shabbat, Chanukah, *Havdalah*, *yahrzeit*, and all the festivals. In consultation with your art teacher, have the students make candles for Shabbat, other special days, and even for use at the synagogue service. Have the students raise money for *tzedakah* by selling their candles (e.g., at the temple gift shop).

2. In the story "Ruth and Naomi," Naomi says to Ruth, "From now on, you must never live in a house that has no *mezuzah* on the door." In consultation with your art teacher, have the students make their own *mezuzot*. (Consider placing within the *mezuzot* not only traditional scriptural texts but individual prayers and wishes that emphasize the spirit of equality.) Teach the students the blessing for affixing *mezuzot* in the classroom or at home: *Baruch Atah, Adonai Eloheinu, Melech haolom, asher kideshanu bemitzvotav vetzivanu likboa mezuzah.*

3. According to "Hannah's Prayer," God is moved to give Hannah a child the same way that a king gives bread to a poor man whose begging goes unheeded. In the spirit of Hannah's prayer, have

the class make sandwiches, gather fruits, and prepare snacks to give to the homeless or have them deliver clothes, toys, and food donated by the synagogue to a women's shelter. If possible organize a class trip to a nursing home, where students will entertain the residents.

FAMILY DISCUSSION ACTIVITIES

1. Encourage the families to follow Deborah's example by studying Torah or other aspects of Jewish studies on a regular basis. Provide the families with questions for discussion on the weekly Torah portion or assign a Torah portion to one family at a time. Have the families prepare the questions and share their answers with the other families in the class.

2. Have the families discuss the following: Jews who convert to Judaism are often referred to as "Jews-by-choice." Ask: "How does the term *Jews-by-choice* differ from the word *converts*?"

3. Have the female members of the family share their feelings about their roles, their responsibilities, and the rewards of being Jewish women.

ANSWER KEY

Activity Book, Chapter 8
Page 36

Deborah's husband's name was **Lappidoth**. Coming home from work very tired, he would not be interested in **studying**. But she tried to encourage him to do **good** deeds. From the wax she collected from **beehives**, Deborah made **candles** for her husband to bring to the **scholars** who studied at **Shiloh**. That is why God called her a "woman of **light**" and chose her to be a **judge**.

9 • KING DAVID STUDIES TORAH

BIOGRAPHIES OF THE TALES' PROTAGONISTS

Before David became king of Israel, he had already displayed remarkable personality traits. He was a dedicated shepherd, as well as a clear-headed, handsome, brave, sensitive, and musically talented young man (I Samuel 16). One moment he was playing soothing harp music for the anguished King Saul, and the next moment he was slaying the fierce Philistine Goliath (I Samuel 17). Initially, David was favored by King Saul whom he served loyally. But as Saul fell deeper and deeper into a state of madness, his admiration for David turned into hatred and jealousy, forcing David to flee for his life. David made efforts at reconciliation with Saul, but these periods of reconciliation were brief. Then Saul resumed his crazed pursuit of David. Not until Saul's death at the hands of the Philistines (I Samuel 31) was David free to take control of the mantle of the country.

David translated his command on the battlefield to his role as earthly ruler of the people, by whom he was beloved and revered. Yet he was not without his weaknesses. His lustful and ruthless pursuit of women is exemplified in the story of Bathsheba (II Samuel 11). But despite David's very human flaws, he is best remembered for his devotion to God. An outstanding example of this dedication was the leadership role he played in transporting the Ark of the Covenant to Jerusalem, thereby creating a spiritual as well as a political capital there. David's devotion is further exemplified by the songs of praise he wrote to God.

BACKGROUND FOR THE TEACHER

The growth of the monarchy in ancient Israel did not progress smoothly. The prophet Samuel was enlisted by the people to help establish an earthly kingship. The Israelites saw that other peoples around them were ruled by kings, and they wanted a king, too. Although Samuel tried to dissuade them, they were determined. So Samuel conferred with God, who told him to "heed their demands and appoint a king for them" (I Samuel 8:22). The first king of ancient Israel was Saul, whom God directed Samuel to anoint. When Saul later failed to follow God's orders, God once again showed Samuel whom to anoint as Saul's successor. This time the anointed was to be David.

The stories in this chapter focus on David, the grandson of Ruth, about whom we read in the last chapter. And the prophet Samuel, who anointed David, was the son of Hannah, who was also mentioned in the previous chapter. The three stories in this chapter paint a multifaceted portrait of David. He was talented, bright, studious, and devoted to God. He spent many hours composing songs of praise to God. For this, tradition attributes to him the authorship of the Book of Psalms. But in "King David Studies Torah" and "David and the Spider," David was also portrayed as egocentric and lacking humility.

In "When Will the Temple Be Built?" we encounter David as a wise, dedicated man of God. However, there are those among the people who tease and taunt him because they are impatient with the delay in the building of the Temple. David ignores their insults and, in the end, agrees with his taunters. Instead of calling them to task for making veiled cries for his death, he joins them in their longing to see the Temple built. (David knew that as man of war his hands could not build the Temple, and so he would have to die before it happened.) To emphasize his sincerity, he refers to this episode in one of his psalms to God.

MOTIVATIONAL ACTION OR STARTER

Explain to the students: Everyone has something in their lives for which they can be proud. Ask the students to complete the following sentence: I am proud of my _____.

Ask for volunteers to share their responses. Tell the class that we are now going to read a story about King David. Ask: "How do you think David would have completed the above sentence."

CLASSROOM DISCUSSION

1. Ask the students: "If you were King David, how would you complete the sentence: I am proud of my _____?" [Possible answers from the story include: my kingship, my city, my harp, my psalms, my voice.] Ask: "Is it possible to have too much pride? Can being proud of your own accomplishments get in the way of seeing the accomplishments of others?"

2. More questions for discussion:

    a. David was inspired by the beauty of the night and the view of his city, Jerusalem, to write a poem of thanks to God, a psalm. An entire book of the Bible called Psalms is filled with 150 poems of praise to God. Ask the students to recall scenes or events that inspired them and have them write a psalm, a poem of thanks to God, about their experience.

    b. The sounds of the night came together to create a song for David. Have the students write their own description of an orchestra or symphony created from sounds in nature (e.g., birds singing like flutes, crickets chirping like cymbals, leaves rustling like violins, frogs croaking like trumpets).

    c. In "King David Studies Torah," the frog asks David, "Is that a proper prayer for a king?… Those are good words for a show-off. But are they good words for a king?" Ask the students: "What do you think? Were they good words for a king? How should a king talk about himself?"

    d. God tells David, "Do not think that any one of My creatures is useless." Have the class give examples of creatures that may appear useless but are not. Have the students explain the merits of the creatures or write a blessing of thanksgiving for the various benefits the creatures provide. [Some suggestions for creatures include: cockroaches, slugs, humming birds, skunks, penguins, jellyfish, bats.]

    e. Ask: "What did King David prove by his reaction to the people who teased him and made him angry? Have you ever ignored teasers? What happened?"

CLASSROOM ACTIVITIES

1. In "King David Studies Torah," we read about the beautiful sounds made on David's harp by the wind. To re-create beautiful sounds, in consultation with your art teacher, have the students make wind chimes from different materials.

2. Over the years, Jews have composed beautiful music for singing in the synagogue. Today many Jews apply new musical styles to familiar words by experimenting with modern melodies. Working with your music teacher, have the students write new words for such familiar Jewish tunes as *David Melech; Al Sheloshah Devarim; Eli,Eli; Maoz Tzur; Mah Nishtanah;* etc.

3. According to the story "When Will the Temple Be Built?" David was not allowed to build the Temple because he was a man of war, and the Temple had to be built by a man of peace. To be a person of peace means following a special code of behavior. Have the class create a list of rules of

behavior expected from those in your temple or classroom. The class list should emphasize qualities that protect people (e.g., "Members and students will not use hurtful language toward one another" or "Members and students shall be tolerant of differences of opinion").

FAMILY DISCUSSION ACTIVITIES

1. Have the families discuss examples of pride in their family. Ask: "What are some things you do as a family that make you proud? What other things can you do to make you proud?"

2. Have the families write their own *berachot*, "blessings," thanking God for creatures and/or elements of nature that are not usually thought of as being useful. In the same vein, have them write *berachot* that thank God for their pets. Tell them to be as creative, serious, or humorous as they like. Compile the *berachot* for distribution at a parents' day or family education day.

ANSWER KEY

Activity Book, Chapter 9
Page 41

King David enjoyed playing the **harp**. One night a **breeze** came through David's window and played on his harp. David listened to the beautiful music and decided to study the **Torah** scroll that was on his table. When the music stopped, David turned from his studies and bragged about how great a **singer** and **scholar** he was. At that moment, **a frog** came to his window and told him not to boast so much since other **animals** could sing even better than he. King David realized that the frog was right, and they spent the rest of the evening singing together, praising God.

Page 44

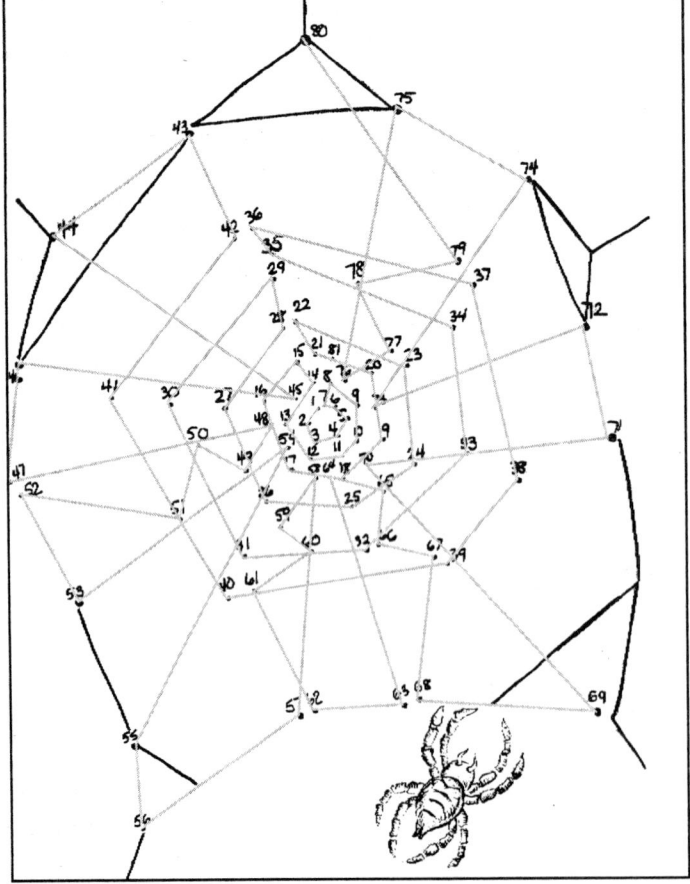

10 • SOLOMON AND THE SNAKE

BIOGRAPHIES OF THE TALES' PROTAGONISTS

King Solomon, the prime character in this chapter, was the son of King David. Solomon succeeded to the throne even before his father's death. Solomon's ascent to the kingship, however, was surrounded by some intrigue when supporters of Adonijah, another of David's sons, tried secretly to anoint Adonijah as king. David's wishes for Solomon to be king, however, were ultimately realized (I Kings 1:32-40).

The biblical accounts of Solomon's reign attribute the peace and prosperity of the era to Solomon's great wisdom. He is described as wiser than all men. He reportedly uttered proverbs and songs; solved riddles; and spoke with the trees, beasts, birds, insects, and fish. One of his greatest attributes was his skill as a wise judge. He did not shrink from the difficult cases brought before him, tackling each one with authority and clarity. Solomon's legacy is so great that tradition ascribes to him the composition of such poetry and works of wisdom as Song of Songs, Proverbs, and Ecclesiastes.

Solomon is closely linked to the Temple. Because his hands, unlike those of David, were not stained by the blood of war, Solomon was given the privilege of overseeing the construction of the Holy Temple in Jerusalem. This tremendous undertaking was carried out under Solomon's watchful eye.

BACKGROUND FOR THE TEACHER

King Solomon and the Temple with which he is so closely associated are the main foci of the stories in this chapter. In "Solomon and the Snake," King Solomon, the son of David, is shown to be a wise man and a master of unraveling difficult disputes when he deftly tackles the case of a man and a thirsty snake. At first glance, Solomon's solution may seem a bit brutal. But on closer examination, we see that it is a good example of the wisdom of Solomon. After hearing the man's description of the case, Solomon establishes his authority by insisting that the snake get down off the man's neck. Solomon then displays his great wisdom by countering the snake's incomplete statement from the Torah with the remainder of the Torah verse, using it as justification for his judgment of the case.

In "Building the Temple," we encounter two very important concepts. The first is the seeming paradox that tools and materials of construction can also be used for destructive purposes. The second is that the Temple was not only a physical place but also a conceptual place. Spaces of peace and light can be built with attitudes and behavior, as well as with concrete materials.

The third story, "God's Special Worm," illustrates Solomon's famous talent for communicating with animals. It also shows how Solomon, who was renowned for his wisdom, appreciated that there was wisdom greater than his own to be learned from God's "simple" creatures.

MOTIVATIONAL ACTION OR STARTER

King Solomon is remembered for being a wise man and a fair judge. He was especially talented at solving difficult disputes. Tell the students that we are now going to read a story about one such dispute. Explain that we will stop before the end of the story to allow them to offer their suggestions for handling the problem presented. Remind them to pay careful attention to all the details.

CLASSROOM DISCUSSION

1. Tell the students to stop reading the story after Solomon says, "Present your case." Ask: "How would you have resolved the dispute?" List the responses on the board and have the students continue the story. Ask the students: "What do you think of Solomon's solution?"

2. More questions for discussion:

    a. The writings from the Torah to which the snake and King Solomon refer come from Genesis 3:15. In this verse, God says to the serpent just after it had tricked Adam and Eve into eating the forbidden fruit, "I will put hatred between you and the woman, and between your offspring and hers; they [people] shall strike at your head, and you [snakes] shall strike at their heel." Ask the students: "After you have read this verse, do you think Solomon was right to have the man in the story strike the snake on the head and kill it? Why? Why not?"

    b. In "Building the Temple," we are reminded that materials can be used both for constructive and destructive purposes. Iron is the example used in this story. Ask the class to provide other examples. Nuclear science has contributed to the creation of both constructive and destructive tools (e.g., nuclear medicine, nuclear energy, and nuclear bombs). Ask the students: "Do you agree or disagree with the following statement: We should avoid using constructive tools because others may misuse them, turning them into instruments of destruction?"

    c. For more puzzle stories, refer to *While Standing on One Foot*, Nina Jaffe and Steve Zeitlin (New York: Henry Holt and Company, 1993). This wonderful collection of seventeen puzzle stories and wisdom tales from the Jewish tradition includes another story about King Solomon.

    d. All that remains of the Second Temple in Jerusalem (the First Temple, built by Solomon, was destroyed in 586 B.C.E. and rebuilt about a hundred years later) is a wall from the outer courtyard. This wall is one of Judaism's holiest sites. Ask the students: "Why do you think Jews consider the wall holy?"

    e. In "God's Special Worm," Solomon says, "People say I am wise but, truly, there is greater wisdom in God's creatures." Ask the students: "What do you think Solomon meant when he made that statement?" Have the students name some creatures in nature from whom they have learned something through observations. Have them describe what they learned.

CLASSROOM ACTIVITIES

1. The construction of the Temple is a very important part of the story "Building the Temple." To teach the importance of the design of a synagogue, take the students on a field trip to the synagogue sanctuary to examine its architecture. Ask the students: "What is the role of light? What makes light important? Are there windows that allow in natural light? Where is the 'eternal light' located? Why is the *bimah* elevated? Can you see the Torah scrolls at all times? In what direction does the temple ark face?" Have the students take notes based on your questions. When they are done, have them return to the classroom to discuss what they have learned. Have the class write an article for the temple newsletter about this expedition.

2. In consultation with your art teacher, have the students construct clay miniature temples with windows that allow the light to come in.

3. According to the story "God's Special Worm," Solomon was not allowed to use metal to build the Temple. The prohibition against using metal to build the Temple is similar to the prohibition concerning the *yad* and the Torah. Take the students on another trip to the synagogue sanctuary

to see the Torah and the *yad*. Explain to the students why the *yad* should not touch the Torah: The *yad* is made of metal, which is also used to make weapons; the Torah is an *etz chayim*, a "tree of life" and peace.

FAMILY DISCUSSION ACTIVITIES

1. In "Building the Temple," we are introduced to the idea that the Temple in Jerusalem was not only a physical place but was also a concept, that is, the Temple was a place of peace. Ask the families: "How can you create a temple of peace in your home? What can you do to make the light in your home an example for others and have it shine out on the world?"

2. Present a challenge to the families: Build a model structure without using metal tools or metal building materials.

3. Ask the members of the family to chose a creature in nature (e.g., insect, bird, or other animal) that they would like to be. Have them explain the reason for their choice.

ANSWER KEY

Activity Book, Chapter 10
Page 46

One day a man met a **thirsty** snake. In exchange for a drink of **milk**, the snake offered to show the man where **money** had been buried. But when the man tried to take the money, the snake tried to **kill** him. However, the man protested and insisted that they both go to **the court** of King Solomon for a decision. Solomon ruled that while the **Torah** says that snakes should kill men, men may also kill snakes. Solomon then handed his **staff** to the man, who used it to kill the snake.

Page 49

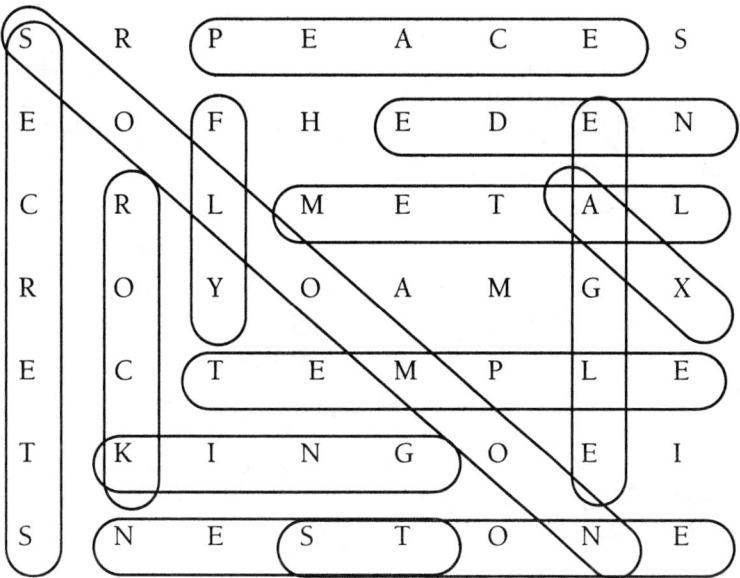

11 • A HUNDRED HIDDEN PROPHETS

BIOGRAPHIES OF THE TALES' PROTAGONISTS

The Israelite prophet Elijah was active during the ninth century B.C.E. He had an almost mystical air about him. The Bible tells us about many unusual episodes in his life, from his success in pleading with God to revive a dead child (I Kings 17) to his supernatural death in a fiery heaven-bound chariot (II Kings 2:11). Above all, Elijah is remembered for his zealous support of the God of Israel, an important example of which is the subject of "A Hundred Hidden Prophets."

The reign of King Ahab and his wife, Jezebel, was marked by the introduction of the religious practices of the cult of Ba'al into the kingdom of Israel. The priests and prophets of Ba'al were said to hold places of honor at Jezebel's table, and a temple of Ba'al was constructed in Samaria, the capital of the northern kingdom of Israel. Elijah could not abide these insults to God. He, therefore, led an opposition movement against the cult of Ba'al and also against the royal family for tolerating the cult's presence in Israel. The height of this confrontation took place on Mount Carmel, where Elijah stood alone challenging the 450 priests of Ba'al. Elijah, firm in his challenge, was victorious because he believed in God, and he believed that God was present with him. He was a model for the other prophets, who did not openly join him in the confrontation but stood loyally united behind him, resisting the urge to go over to the side of the enemy.

BACKGROUND FOR THE TEACHER

The stories in this chapter are linked by their common historical juxtaposition. They all take place after the reign of King Solomon. After Solomon's death, the kingdom that David and Solomon had worked so vigorously to build fell victim to the clash of wills between Rehoboam and Jeroboam. These two sons of Solomon fought to determine who should succeed their father. The result was the secession of the northern region, which came to be known as the kingdom of Israel. It encompassed ten of the twelve tribes and was led by Jeroboam. The southern region, known as the kingdom of Judah, included the remaining two tribes and was led by Rehoboam. The division of the kingdom led to a long series of ups and downs. Some rulers took an aggressive approach toward their neighbors; others were more conciliatory. Some rulers were steadfast in their commitment to the ways and traditions of the Israelites; others lost touch with the past of their people. The stories in this chapter give us some glimpses into this era.

"A Hundred Hidden Prophets" begins with a reference to the division of the kingdom into two parts. Then it details the reign of Ahab, king of Israel. According to scholars, Ahab pursued peaceful relations with his neighbors, but in the Bible (I Kings 16:33), we read that he "did more to vex *Adonai*, the God of Israel, than all the kings of Israel who preceded him." Chief among his wrongdoings was allowing his wife, Jezebel, to bring the pagan practices of the worship of Ba'al into the kingdom of Israel. This blatant disloyalty precipitated the creation of an opposition movement led by the prophet Elijah. Elijah's confrontation with the priests of Ba'al confirmed the greater might of the God of Israel and caused the people to renew their commitment to God (I Kings 18).

The kingdom of Israel, however, was not to last long. It fell at the hands of the Assyrians (II Kings 17), and all the inhabitants were sent into exile. The Bible states that they met this fate because they "had sinned against *Adonai* their God…. They had worshiped other gods" (II Kings 17:7). The dispersion of the ten tribes, whose fate remains a mystery to this day, is the focus of "Like This Day…." In this story, the rabbis address the question of whether or not the tribes will ever return to the Land of Israel. In characteristic rabbinic fashion, the story offers two opinions but does not give a definitive answer.

In "Hezekiah and Manasseh," we touch on the reigns of two kings in the southern kingdom of Judah. Hezekiah and then his son, Manasseh, carried out their responsibilities in vastly different fashions. Each ruler stands as an example. The former is a model of dedication to God; the latter is a prime illustration of disregard for the wisdom and teachings of the past. To appreciate the contrast, we are enjoined to remember both Hezekiah and Manasseh.

MOTIVATIONAL ACTION OR STARTER

Make four signs, each bearing one of the following statements:

1. Loyalty is undying devotion to a person or thing.
2. Loyalty is standing by a friend or family member, right or wrong.
3. Loyalty is sincere only if backed up by words and actions.
4. Loyalty to God is the highest form of loyalty.

Place the four signs in the four corners of the room. Ask the students to stand next to the sign they think best reflects their idea of loyalty. Ask for volunteers to explain the reason for their choice. Students may move from one corner to another if they are swayed by the remarks of another class member. (Students who are unsure of the corner in which they want to stand may stand in the middle of the room. The students in the four corners should try to convince those in the middle of the wisdom of the sign in their corner and encourage those in the middle to come to that corner.)

After the students have completed the above activity, tell them that we are now going to read a story in which loyalty is a key theme. Ask: "Do the four-corner statements apply to our story?"

CLASSROOM DISCUSSION

1. Ask the students: "Which of the four-corner definitions applies to Elijah? Which applies to the hundred hidden prophets? Which applies to the Israelite soldiers who fought in war under Ahab?"

2. More questions for discussion:

    a. Elijah created an opposition movement to the royal family and the priests of Ba'al. Ask the students which of the following wrongdoings of Ahab and Jezebel was the most terrible:

    Jezebel brought idols and the priests of Ba'al (a pagan god) into Israel.

    Ahab built temples for the priests of Ba'al.

    Ahab destroyed the altar of God.

    Ahab and Jezebel compromised their loyalty to God.

    b. Except for Elijah, all the prophets of Israel feared Ahab. They thought Ahab's victories in three wars proved that God supported him. Tell the students to imagine themselves as one of the hidden prophets. From the list below, have the students choose the reason they believe was responsible for Ahab's victories:

    Ahab was a strong leader.

    The Israelites were good and loyal soldiers.

    God was on Ahab's side.

c. The unwillingness of the hundred hidden prophets to support King Ahab and the priests of Ba'al was the equivalent of a silent protest. Ask the students if they agree or disagree with this statement.

d. Ask the students: "How important is loyalty to you? To which of the following would you say you are most loyal: your family, your school, your town, your country, your people (other Jews), or God?"

e. In "Like This Day...," we read two opinions on the question of whether or not the ten lost tribes will ever return to the Land of Israel. But we do not get a final answer. Have the students choose either the opinion of Rabbi Akiva or Rabbi Eliezer for a class debate.

f. There are many stories about what happened to the ten lost tribes. One story states that the Jews of Ethiopia are descendants of the ten lost tribes. For a time, a popular theory claimed that the Native Americans were the ten tribes that disappeared after the kingdom of Israel was conquered by the Assyrians. Have the students write their own creative explanation for what happened to these tribes after they were defeated and exiled.

g. In the story "Hezekiah and Manasseh," we read that we are to remember both the teachings of Hezekiah and the sins of Manasseh. Ask the students: "Why do you think we are supposed to remember both?"

CLASSROOM ACTIVITIES

1. In the story "A Hundred Hidden Prophets," Elijah showed his bravery by standing up to Jezebel and the priests of Ba'al. This act of bravery makes Elijah a Jewish hero. Have the students create a wall of heroes in the classroom. The heroes should be those who stood up against injustice and united to defeat evil. Have the students look for these heroes in magazines, newspapers, and even comic books. Have the students cut out pictures of and text about these heroes and make a collage on poster board. Consult your art teacher for details.

2. The story "Like This Day..." teaches us about the dispersion of Israel's people and our hope for their return to Israel. To explore the tension between these two images of the Jewish people, bring a flag of Israel and an American flag into the classroom, as well as recordings of the American and Israeli national anthems ("The Star Spangled Banner" and "Hativkah"). Ask the students which anthem should be sung first. Have them explain their answer. Then ask the students to create their own version of an American and an Israeli flag using simple materials like paper and colored pens. Have the students discuss why they chose to redesign the flags the way they did, reflecting their own sense of what it means to be Jewish and American.

3. The Judean king Hezekiah had a great deal of trouble with his son, Manasseh, who preferred idol worship to Torah study. Discuss the thorny issue of what parents expect from their children. Select three students to play the roles of two parents and their child. Have them dramatize an argument between the parents and the child about the child's having to attend Hebrew school. Have individual students "freeze" the action and replace one of the participants in the argument. When the role-play is completed, ask the students to compare the role-play with the story of Hezekiah and Manasseh. Ask: "Are there any solutions to the conflict between the arguing parents and child?"

FAMILY DISCUSSION ACTIVITIES

1. Have the families discuss the following: King Solomon devoted much time, energy, and resources to building a strong kingdom, but his sons were the cause for its collapse into two smaller,

weaker kingdoms. Hezekiah was a model king, but his son was just the opposite. Ask the families to explain why they think parents and children can be so different. Have them give other examples—including ones where children outshine their parents.

2. Another family discussion topic: Manasseh questioned why he should pay attention to the words and wisdom of the past. Ask: "How do parents convey the value of past wisdom to their children?" Tell the families to look around their house for objects that are reminders of the past.

ANSWER KEY

Activity Book, Chapter 11
Page 51

After the reign of King **Solomon**, Israel was divided into the kingdoms of **Judah** and Israel. The king of Israel was named **Ahab**, and he married a woman named Jezebel. She was a wicked queen and brought **idols** into the Temple and the priests of **Ba'al** into the country. At that time, there were **a hundred** prophets in Israel. When they all went into **hiding**, only the prophet **Elijah** spoke out against Jezebel.

Page 53

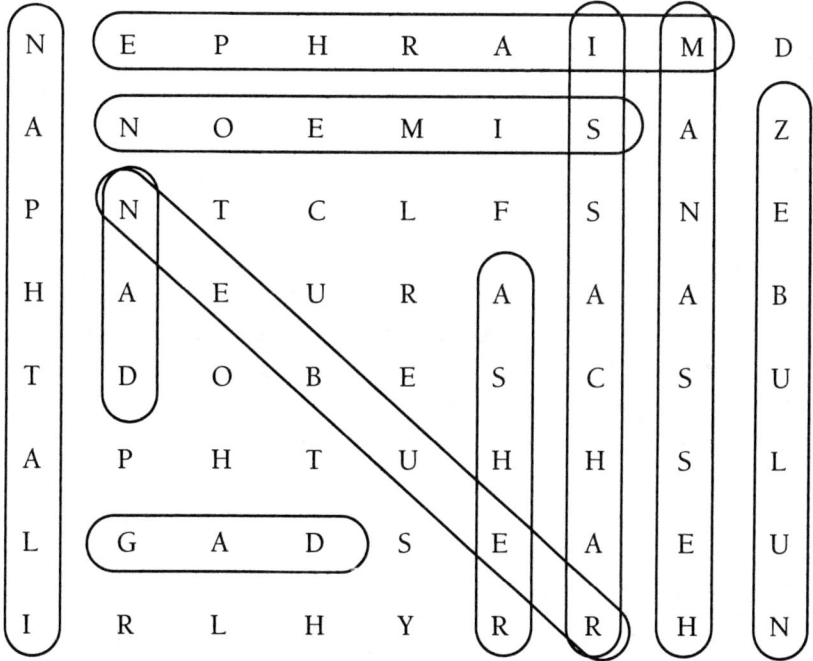

12 • JEREMIAH AND MOSES

BIOGRAPHIES OF THE TALES' PROTAGONISTS

The first story of this chapter brings together Moses and Jeremiah, two of the greatest leaders in Jewish history. While we might not immediately think to pair them, their biographies share several similarities. They were both chosen by God to serve as messengers to the Jewish people. The Bible reports that both initially responded to God's call by declaring themselves unworthy of the responsibility. Yet both served God and the Jewish people in exemplary fashion. They also shared a role in leading the Jewish people during watershed events in our history: Moses, of course, led us out of Egypt, through the wilderness to the Promised Land. Jeremiah lived and prophesied during the period leading up to and including the exile to Babylonia. Finally, both Moses and Jeremiah were challenged to constantly renew the people's spirits and their sense of commitment to God's law.

The central message of "Jeremiah and Moses" that God is too great to merely be localized in the Temple in Jerusalem is one that Jeremiah stressed. After the exile he sought to console and strengthen the exiles with the message that their relationship with God could and must continue outside the Land of Israel, beyond the confines of the Temple site.

BACKGROUND FOR THE TEACHER

In this chapter, we encounter one of the most shattering events in Jewish history: the destruction of the southern kingdom of Judah at the hands of the Babylonians and the exile that followed. Starting with the Exodus from Egypt, the Bible focuses on our desire to return to the land promised us by God. The vast majority of our tale, as reported in the Bible, is devoted to the story of our struggle to settle and hold onto the Land of Israel once we got there. In the Book of Jeremiah, we come to the end of our autonomy over the southern kingdom of Judah (the northern kingdom of Israel having fallen earlier to the Assyrians) and the resultant trauma, the exile. In the face of exile, Jewish continuity was the most important issue to the prophet Jeremiah, and continuity is the common thematic thread that runs through the stories in this chapter. Whether the question posed is how could (can) Judaism and the Jewish people survive in exile or how could (can) Jews survive the evil plans of an enemy like Haman, these stories focus on how we do manage to continue as a people. And the answer is two-sided: To ensure a Jewish future, God must will it, *and* we must work to sustain an enduring commitment to God.

In "Jeremiah and Moses," God abandons the Temple in Jerusalem only after receiving the assurance that the people will be consoled and emboldened by the spirits of the great leaders of the past. Only after Moses, Abraham, Sarah, Isaac, Rebecca, Jacob, Rachel, and Leah gather to mourn the loss of the Temple does God feel comfortable leaving the Temple. This story stresses that buildings do not hold God's spirit and move us forward as a people; but by having a sense of connection to the Jewish past, we are motivated to become links to a Jewish future.

The "Three Prophets" addresses the very concrete question of how to survive in exile. Although the answers are given in poetic terms, they are, in fact, very pragmatic. Knowledge of ritual, prayer, and education of the young have been and always will be essential to our survival as a people.

God's reciprocal role in assuring our continuity emerges in both the first and third stories of this chapter. In "Jeremiah and Moses," God tells the angels, "My people cannot be destroyed." In "Foolish Haman," the plan to destroy the Jews is described as being as senseless as a bird's plan to change the sea into dry land and the dry land into sea. According to this story, God's protection saved us from the foolish plans of a foolish man.

MOTIVATIONAL ACTION OR STARTER

Ask the class to imagine where God lives and describe the image they have. After you have the students' responses, tell them that we are now going to read a story about the great prophets Jeremiah and Moses, which takes place at the time of the destruction of the Temple in Jerusalem in 586 B.C.E. Point out that they are to pay attention to how the story addresses the question of where God lives.

CLASSROOM DISCUSSION

1. In Chapter 10, we read about the great care King Solomon took in building the Temple. In the Bible, the Temple is called the house of God. In the fourth year of Solomon's reign over Israel, he built the house of God (I Kings 9). And in this chapter, in "Jeremiah and Moses," we read that the angels asked, "Can the Temple be destroyed? Can human beings ruin the place where God dwells?" Ask the students: "If the Temple was truly God's house, how was it destroyed? Where did God dwell after the destruction of the Temple? Where does God live today?"

2. More questions for discussion:

    a. When God tells Jeremiah to cry out to Moses, the prophet replies, "O God, no one knows where You buried Moses." In Deuteronomy 34, we read about the death of Moses, and the Bible states that no one knows where Moses is buried. Ask the students: "What explanation can you give for this? What if we did know the location of Moses' grave?"

    b. When Moses heard that the Temple was to be destroyed, he ripped the sleeve of his robe. Tearing one's clothes (or in modern times, wearing an article of clothing or a ribbon that has been cut) is a sign of mourning. Ask: "What do you think is the meaning of this custom?"

    c. The story "Jeremiah and Moses" ends with God saying, "Now I can leave the Temple and let it die. The Children of Israel will hear words of comfort from their leaders." Ask the students: "Who are the leaders today that offer comfort when we face times of crisis as a people?"

    d. Have the students make a list of what they think are the most important things to remember about the Jewish past.

    e. Throughout Jewish history, there has been a distinction made between living in the Land of Israel and living outside it. Ask: "In what ways do you think your life differs from the life of the Jews living in modern Israel today?"

    f. In both the story "Foolish Haman" and *Megillat Esther*, the "Scroll of Esther," which we read on Purim, it is said that the Jewish people were saved by Mordecai and Esther. God is not even directly mentioned in *Megillat Esther*. Ask the students: "What role do you think God played? What 'proof' can you bring either from the Purim story or from the story 'Foolish Haman'?"

CLASSROOM ACTIVITIES

1. Like the leaders of Israel, whose words will comfort the Jewish people, we, too, can comfort a family or religious school classmate who is sad, ill, or in mourning by providing a care package. Have the students use the *midrash* about the prophets as inspiration to make care packages of

food, magazines, flowers, comic books, etc., to bring good cheer to someone in a time of despair.

2. From the "Three Prophets," we learn the importance of remembering to maintain our identity. Ask the students to tell the rest of the class memorable stories told to them by their parents or grandparents. Then ask the students to tell stories of events in their own lives that they would like to pass on to their children. When the storytelling is done, have the students create a scroll of remembrance that includes the stories they have told. Have them dedicate the scroll on a Friday night or Saturday morning during Shabbat services.

3. Although the Book of Esther is a story about an evil leader's failed attempt to destroy the Jews, we reenact the story in a humorous way to remind us of the importance of laughter. The merry-making of Purim is often expressed by a *purimspiel*, a funny play about the story of Esther. Have your class write its own *purimspiel*, emphasizing the importance of humor in responding to the violent desires of others.

FAMILY DISCUSSION ACTIVITIES

1. Have the families discuss: The "Three Prophets" addresses the very central matter of what Jews must do to survive. Although presented in poetic terms, the answers are, in fact, very concrete. Below are interpretations of the three answers:

    a. Knowledge of Jewish rituals and how to perform them.

    b. Commitment to prayer.

    c. Education of the younger members of our community.

    Ask the students: "Which answer do you think is the most important? Why? What would you add to the list?"

2. Have the family members share their dreams for the Jewish future. Ask the families: "Where will Jews live? How will they practice Judaism? How will they educate themselves?"

ANSWER KEY

Activity Book, Chapter 12
Page 56

When the Temple was about to be destroyed by the **Babylonians**, God commanded his prophet **Jeremiah** to summon Moses by calling out Moses' name from the banks of the river **Jordan**. When Moses appeared, he was informed that the Temple was to be destroyed. Moses then summoned the spirits of the **matriarchs** and **patriarchs**. Together they went to the **gates** of the Temple, their heads bent in **sorrow**. Only after God was certain that the Jews would hear words of **comfort** from their leaders was the Temple destroyed.

Notes

Notes